A CeNTuRy
OF CHANGE

Communications

Jane Shuter

Heinemann
LIBRARY

First published in Great Britain by Heinemann Library,
Halley Court, Jordan Hill, Oxford OX2 8EJ
a division of Reed Educational and Professional
Publishing Ltd.
Heinemann is a registered trademark of Reed Educational
& Professional Publishing Ltd.

OXFORD MELBOURNE AUCKLAND
JOHANNESBURG BLANTYRE GABORONE
IBADAN PORTSMOUTH (NH) USA CHICAGO

Designed by Celia Floyd
Originated by Ambassador
Printed in Hong Kong

04 03 02 01 00
10 9 8 7 6 5 4 3 2 1

ISBN 0 431 03888 0
This title is also available in a hardback library edition
(ISBN 0 431 03881 3).

British Library Cataloguing in Publication Data

Shuter, Jane
    Communications. – (A century of change)
    1. Communication – Great Britain – History – 19th
      century – Juvenile literature
    2. Communication – Great Britain – History – 20th
      century – Juvenile literature
    I. Title
    384'.0941'09034

Acknowledgements
The Publishers would like to thank the following for
permission to reproduce photographs:

Bridgeman Art Library, p. 26; Bob Rowan/Progressive
Image/Corbis, p. 5; British Film Institute, p. 18; Corbis-
Bettman, pp. 10, 12, 24; Hulton Getty, pp. 20, 22; ITN,
p. 17; Mary Evans Picture Library, p. 16; Minnesota
Histoical Society/Corbis, p. 6; Nokia, p. 9; Popperfoto, p.
19; Robert Harding Picture Library, p. 23; Roger
Scruton, p. 21; Science Museum/Science and Society
Picture Library, pp. 8, 14; Science Photo Library, pp. 13,
15, 27, 28, 29; Telegraph Colour Library, p. 25; The Post
Office, pp. 4, 7.

Cover photograph reproduced with permission of Science
Museum/Science and Society Picture Library and Nokia.

Our thanks to Becky Vickers for her help in the
preparation of this book.

Every effort has been made to contact copyright holders
of any material reproduced in this book. Any omissions
will be rectified in subsequent printings if notice is given
to the Publisher.

For more information about Heinemann Library books,
or to order, please telephone +44 (0)1865 888066, or
send a fax to +44 (0)1865 314091. You can visit our
website at www.heinemann.co.uk

Any words appearing in the text in bold, **like this**, are
explained in the glossary.

CONTENTS

Person to person

Everyone needs to communicate. We need to make contact with other people to learn, exchange information, make business deals, even just to chat. In 1900 there were far fewer methods of communication than there are now. Most people communicated face to face with the people they saw regularly, saving up news or information until their next meeting.

At a distance

If people did not meet regularly then there was really only one way to stay in touch – by letter.

By 1900 a combination of railways and **steamships** made the postal service seem amazingly fast. Letters sent abroad reached their destination about five times faster in 1900 than in 1850. By 1900 letters were being delivered inside the UK for just the cost of a stamp. People used the post more, and so more post offices sprang up.

In 1900 there were newly invented means of communication that were spreading fast. Telephones were becoming increasingly widespread, but were still not in common use. The **telegraph** connected countries worldwide but it was expensive to use. You had to pay for each word you used, so people only used it for short messages.

The London Sorting Office in 1907. The mail was all sorted by hand.

An even wider range

We now have an ever-expanding range of ways to communicate. Most of this communication is done electronically, much of it using the telephone lines. We can send messages by phone, **fax** or **e-mail**. We can look for information on the Internet, using computers. We can put information there, too. We can even use the Internet to communicate 'face to face' using a video system that sends images directly to the other person or people.

A phone in every home?

Now phones are used all over the world. They are especially common in **developed countries**. Here are some examples of how many homes have a phone and had one in 1900:

	Now	1900
UK	97%	under 1%
USA	99%	1.5%
Australia	98%	under 1%
Ghana	1%	no records
Bangladesh	under 1%	no records

Instant contact

Modern communication is almost instant. People can be in touch with someone on the other side of the world in the same time as it would take them to walk into the next room to talk to a member of their family! They are usually in touch as soon as they have dialled a telephone number, or typed in an e-mail or Internet address.

The children in this school can use computers to help with their school work.

A quick delivery

In 1900 letters were the most effective way of keeping in touch, and in some cases the postal service was faster than it is now! This was partly because there were several deliveries a day. Also, letters were sorted by hand in local **sorting offices**, so local post was often delivered the same day, especially in large towns and cities. So, in London it was possible to post a letter in the morning and have a reply by early afternoon (if the person who got the letter replied straight away).

Rail delivery in the USA and UK was speeded up by sorting letters on trains. Each little wooden box is for a different location. The workers opened sacks of letters and sorted them by hand.

Circling the world

Letters sent abroad took longer than they do now. There was no airmail delivery, so all letters were carried by sea. The most advanced **steamship** could cross the Atlantic in five days. Letters then had to be sorted, and delivered to their destination. A letter posted from London to New York could well be delivered in just over a week. One sent from London to Sydney would take about ten weeks. But sorting and delivering inside a country still took time. So if a letter was posted in a country village in the UK, and had to go to a small village in a state in the American mid-west, it could take between four and five weeks to get there.

Covering the world

Now most letters and parcels can be sent by airmail. This cuts down the amount of time they take to arrive. An airletter will get from the UK to Australia in about five days. Very heavy things (such as furniture) have to go by sea or land. Because sea travel takes longer (about six to eight weeks for the same destinations) it is cheaper, and so is useful even for light mail that is not urgent.

Today, mail is sorted electronically using computers.

Getting better?

In 1900 people wrote letters more regularly than they do now. Today people prefer to pick up the telephone and chat, or use **e-mail**. Much of the post that people get today are bills and other non-personal letters, including junk mail. Post services keep cutting down their staff numbers, mostly because they now have machines to do many of the jobs people used to do, such as sorting letters. Many local sorting offices have been closed, too. This means that local post has to go to the nearest sorting office (often many kilometres away in the nearest big town) and then come back to be delivered!

More people

Fewer people send letters today but there are now far more homes in the world to deliver mail to. For example, the population of the UK in 1900 was about 37 million. It is now about 54 million – and many of these people live separately rather than in large family groups. So there are about 15 million more homes to send letters to. Many countries have developed area codes to help the postal services to sort the letters accurately – for example, zip codes in the USA, and postcodes in the UK.

An instant success?

The telephone was invented in 1876 at almost the same time, by both Elisha Grey and Alexander Graham Bell. Both inventors were living in the USA. It was the first easy-to-use device for speaking over long distances. It was clear the telephone would be incredibly useful. People rushed to study the design and to improve it. In 1878, in the USA, Thomas Edison improved both the **transmitter** that sent the sound and the **receiver** that picked it up; his changes meant messages could be sent across distances of kilometres, rather than just a few metres.

The telephone took off most rapidly in the USA. By 1887 about 30,000 homes and businesses in the USA, and about 12,000 homes and businesses in Britain, had telephones.

Jobs for women?

The telephone opened up a whole new range of jobs. First, the basic telephone system had to be built involving construction workers and engineers. Once set up it also needed engineers to keep it running. While most of the telephone company's workers were men, most of the telephone **operators** were women. Tests showed that most people responded better to a female voice!

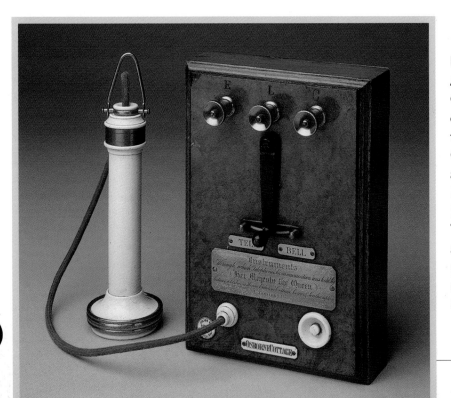

In 1878 Alexander Graham Bell demonstrated the telephone to Queen Victoria at Osborne House on the Isle of Wight. This telephone and terminal panel is the one she contacted at Osborne Cottage.

A different system

Most modern homes, especially in **developed countries**, have telephones (about 28 million in the UK). Modern exchanges are **automatic**, so people only call operators if they are having trouble reaching the number they want. Calls to other countries travel through undersea wires, many using **fibre optics** or, more often, are sent as signals that are bounced off **satellites** in space.

Look, no wires!

Mobile (cellular) phones are very important to modern life. Many people want to be able to get in touch with other people at all times. More than 50 million Americans, about 1 in 5, have a mobile phone. These phones send signals to base stations that send them on to the right destination. Portable phones have become so popular, so fast, that it can be hard to make a call on one because all the lines from the base station are being used. (This is what happened in the early days of the telephone!) So scientists are now working on using small satellites to act as base stations.

They will be able to serve far wider areas, and reach isolated places that are not covered at all at the moment. Parts of the world that have never been connected by **terrestrial** phones will be able to use this system.

Mobile telephone companies are working hard to develop phones that are smaller and lighter than the last.

The latest thing!

The telephone system in 1900 was very slow. First the person making a call had to ring the **operator** in their local telephone **exchange**. They told the operator the number they wanted. If they were calling a local number, the operator called the person being phoned. If the phone call was being made to another part of the country the operator had to go through another exchange, or more than one, to reach the local exchange of the person being phoned. This exchange then made the connection.

Getting connected could often take 15-20 minutes. Phoning overseas took even longer. People told the operator the number they wanted and the operator phoned back once the connection was made. It could take days.

Better and better

By 1901, some places even had **automated** telephone exchanges. These were invented by a US undertaker called Almon Strowger in 1889. He wanted people to be able to contact him directly to arrange funerals, rather than have to talk to an operator first.

In the 1900s all telephone calls had to go through **switchboard** operators.

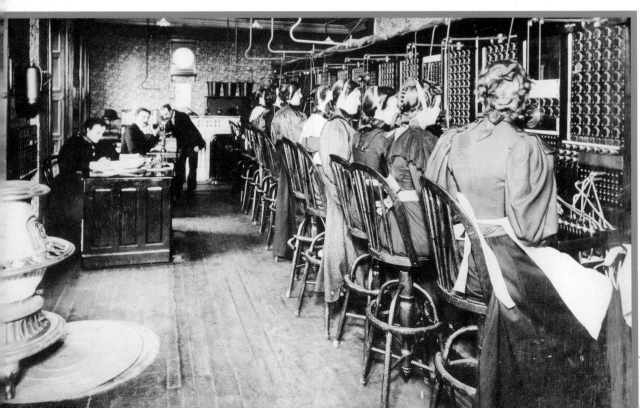

More than just a phone

Telephone lines are now used to do many other things than just relay conversations. They can be linked up to computers or other machines to send **faxes** and **e-mail**. **ISDN** links use telephone lines to send long written messages, even books, from one computer to another. They are so fast that it is possible for people on two different computers to see this text and work on it together on their computer screens.

Home and away

In 1998 the phone company, British Telecom, suggested that in the new millennium it will be possible for ordinary people to use telephones that send digitized images to the home computer. This will use the same techniques as the conferencing techniques that exist now but are very expensive. It will allow family members who are away from home to speak face to face with their family.

Most modern telephone exchanges are computerized and allow calls to be put through instantly.

Spanning the world

A **telegraph** line is a wire running above ground or under the sea, along which messages, called telegrams, are sent electrically a letter at a time. They are sent using a code. The most widely used code was **Morse Code**, invented in the USA in 1837 by Samuel Morse.

The telegraph could link people and places without a telephone. People could send a message and get a reply fast, sometimes in less than an hour.

Telegraph users

Most people used the telegraph to send essential, short messages that had to be sent quickly. People did not use the telegraph to chat because of the cost (they had to pay for each word they used).

This man is using Morse Code to send a telegram.

Networks and connections

Today, very few people send telegrams. The Internet uses the latest technology to send words and pictures from one computer to another along telephone lines. People with special **ISDN** telephone lines can link computers to work on the same document, even if they are miles apart. Systems like these, where computers send the information to each other **digitally**, as strings of codes made up of the numbers 0 and 1, makes sending and receiving much faster.

The Internet

People can use the Internet to research almost any subject and to make contact with other people with the same interests. More and more shops are using the Internet to sell goods. Politicians are using it to put across their views to people.

Many web sites have 'chat rooms' that people can visit to 'talk' to other people all around the world. People can set up 'home pages' (their own information pages) about anything they want. There is even a home page that runs all day showing a woman in the USA, called Jenny, going about her everyday life. She is filmed on cameras set up all around her flat.

These people are using a personal computer to look at a page on the Internet.

Signals without wires

In 1895 the inventor Guglielmo Marconi, working in the USA, sent electrical signals from a **transmitter** to a **receiver** without wires by making sparks jump to create **electromagnetic** waves of sound.

At first Marconi could only send his signal from a transmitter to a receiver 9 metres away. But in 1901 he sent his first signal across the Atlantic Ocean to Britain. At this stage **Morse Code** was used and, just like the **telegraph**, only individual letters could be sent.

How was it used?

As early as 1897 companies that made **wireless equipment** for scientists and big organizations also sold it to the public. Some ordinary people were interested enough in the idea of radio to buy the materials to make their own wireless sets. But the sets were hard to assemble, complicated to use and did not cover long distances. At first, the main users of wireless radio were organizations, such as the police and navy, who used it to send short messages. As its range increased, radio became more important for sending messages at sea.

Radio waves

Radio waves are a kind of electromagnetic waves, just as light and X-rays are. The speed at which they are sent can be varied. This is called the **frequency**. There are lots of frequencies used to send different sorts of information.

Marconi sent the first radio signals across the Atlantic using this transmitter.

More and more signals

Once Marconi developed the wireless transmitter, rapid advances in technology meant that radios could be made that worked better and cost less. In 1915 the American Telephone and Telegraph Company sent a message from the USA to France using whole words that could be recognized as speech. Now that sounds could be sent, the radio quickly became used for entertainment. By the 1920s, there were 50 million radios in use in the USA alone. Modern radios can use a much wider range of frequencies to send out music and speech. Also, radios can be made so tiny that they can fit onto an earpiece.

Different uses

Radios provide people with entertainment and news. People can also use radio transmitters to send each other their own messages using Citizens' Band (CB) frequencies. Certain frequencies are only used by the emergency services and have to be left clear for them.

Reaching out further

There are still some parts of the world that do not have access to electricity supplies. This is usually because they are hard to reach or people cannot afford to pay the price. However, there are radios that do not need electricity and work on human power – you turn a handle on the side of the radio to create the power needed to work it. They were invented partly to solve this problem, by the British inventor Trevor Baylis. Baylis went on to invent a wind-up clock and a wind-up torch. Wind-up radios need winding up over and over again. But they do let people in remote places have contact with other places around the world.

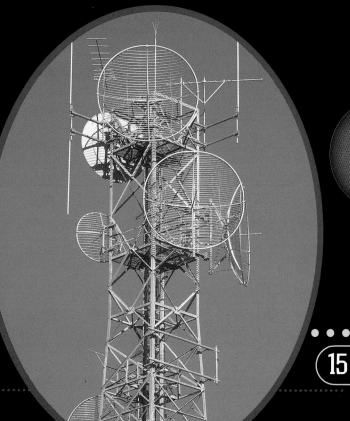

Large radio transmitters are used to send radio waves over huge distances.

Moving pictures

Moving pictures quickly became popular. The first movies were just films of waves on the beach or people dancing. They only lasted a few minutes. But by 1900 there were movies that told stories. By 1909, the movie business was making about $40 million and employing 100,000 people, compared to a few hundred in 1900. In 1906 the first full-length feature film was made in Australia. It was called *Story of the Kelly Gang*.

But film was useful for more than just telling stories. For the first time, people could see film of news events as they happened. News films were often shown at cinemas before or after the movie.

What about sound?

Early movies were silent. Written conversations or explanations of the storyline were put in between scenes. Many cinemas employed pianists to play music to go with what was happening in the film.

'Talkies'

The first movie to have talking as well as music was *The Jazz Singer*, made in 1927. The famous silent movie star Charlie Chaplin, thought talkies would not last. But the movie magazine *Film Spectator* remarked: '*If I were an actor with a squeaky voice, I would worry.*'

This early newsreel shows a boat race and the crowds that came to watch it.

Bigger and better?

It has become so much easier for people to watch movies at home on TV or video, that movie-makers have to try hard to get people to go to the cinema to watch movies. They make films that have special effects that will look better on a large screen; they spend a great deal of money on films and publicize the fact; they employ stars who charge a lot of money; they do all these things to make people want to watch the movie in the cinema as soon as it comes out.

In 1998 the film *Titanic* cost $200 million to make. This was more money than any other movie had cost before. But it made more money too, over $1 billion.

Cinemas have become a place purely for entertainment. They do not show news reports anymore. Some cinemas have several smaller cinemas under one roof, all showing different movies.

The film *Independence Day* used incredible special effects to try to attract audiences to the cinema.

The way newspapers are produced has changed greatly since 1900.

Getting the news

In 1900 most of the news was collected by reporters. The reporters had to get their news stories in to their paper as quickly as possible. They telephoned in their reports, dictating them to an editor in the newspaper office. If they could not reach a phone they sent a telegram, but this would only contain the basic facts.

Printing the news

Printing newspapers was a long business. Pictures were drawn as **engravings**. A colour one took four days to get ready, a black and white one took two days.

The words were set in **type**, a letter at a time. The type was set into blocks, and put together to make the columns of text. The printer had to put each letter into the right block, one by one. The letters had to be back to front so that they would print the right way round. Once the type had been **set** any changes were very time-consuming.

The set pages were then run over an ink roller and covered in just the right amount of ink. Then sheets of paper were run over them, on rollers, going as fast as they could while still getting a clear **impression** of all the words.

This photograph taken in 1890 shows the presses used to print newspapers. By 1900, over a thousand sheets an hour could be run off.

Getting the news

Most news is still collected by reporters. But today they often send their news in by portable computer using **ISDN** lines. They use computer technology as much as possible because today newspapers are mainly produced on computers.

Printing the news

Photographs, pictures and diagrams, black and white and colour, can be sent as **digital** images to a newspaper editor.

The text is written and laid out on computer too, and the pictures are dropped in and shifted until they are the right size and in the right place. It is easy to change text and move it around, and even replace it at the last minute with a whole new story. This means that news and pictures reach the reader much more quickly after the event than they did in 1900.

Today's newspaper companies can produce colour magazines or supplements quickly and cheaply using computers.

Propaganda is the spreading of opinions or ideas, especially biased or false ones, in the hope of getting others to believe them. Propaganda can be communicated in many ways. Television, film, radio and newspapers are the most obvious and often the most widespread.

War propaganda

Between 1900 and 2000 film has often been used as propaganda, especially in wartime.

Governments have wanted to show the enemy as bad, and themselves as the winning side. Film propaganda was first used in the First World War (1914–18). Film-makers had to be careful not to show anything too horrific – their films were checked by the government. Many historians think that public opinion would have swung against the war sooner if people had been shown the real conditions and battles.

This is a photograph of the Battle of the Somme 1916. If the general public had seen pictures of what was really happening on the battlefields they may not have backed the war for so long.

News reporting

Today, most film reports of war and famines are shown on TV, but they can still be propaganda. When people see the victims of civil wars in Africa, it is hard to feel any sympathy for the people who are hurting the victims even if they, too, have their own horror stories to tell.

No rules?

Film is not the only way of spreading propaganda. The Internet can reach people on a global scale. But because the Internet has sprung up and expanded rapidly, there are no government rules to govern how it is used as yet.

Anyone with the right equipment can use the Net and even set up their own home pages. In this way people can spread their own propaganda throughout the world. The lack of government control over the Internet means that there is no way of checking the accuracy of information provided by sites on the Net, nor of checking that people are who they say they are. Many people want governments to impose regulations. Governments point out that it would be hard to set up regulations governing something that is quite so easily accessed which would work world-wide.

Pictures, like this, of refugee camps in Africa have caused international aid projects because people are made more aware of events happening in other parts of the world.

Most ordinary forms of communication do not need to be kept secret from other people. But some groups, such as government spies, criminals and the police, need a language that only they can understand.

Visible signals

Armies and navies were using visible signals long before any form of radio communication was invented. In 1900 they could send signals from group to group or ship to ship by flashing lights, or hanging out various flags. The signals gave orders about where to go or what to do in battle. But these signals only worked if the people sending the messages were in sight of each other.

The prisoners in this chain gang would have had their own language code, a kind of slang, so that other people could not understand them.

Special languages

Written messages could travel further, but they were in danger of falling into enemy hands. So they had to be written in a secret language or **code**. Early codes were quite simple, such as giving each letter of the alphabet a number and writing out a long list of numbers as the message. But these codes were quite easy to work out. So people began to work out more complicated codes.

Stealing secrets

Countries at war, or on the brink of war, want to get hold of each other's plans and secrets. In 1900 the only way to do this was for a spy to break into the place where the documents were kept and steal them, copy them out, or learn them by heart.

Machines and gadgets

Spying is much easier now. A great deal of information is stored on computers. People who are very skilled at using computers can **'hack'** into these computers even if protected by a series of passwords. They can steal secrets without even leaving home. There is no need to break into buildings. In the 1990s there were several incidents where hackers got into the computers that ran the US defence systems.

Robot spies

Governments also take advantage of special communication systems, such as **satellites**, to spy on other countries. Satellites can take pictures from space that are so detailed they can pick out individual people. But most countries know about the spy satellites. In 1998 Indian engineers who were working on nuclear missile testing managed to evade discovery by spy satellites. They knew when the satellites would be passing over and hid any evidence of their activity at that time.

All on a microchip?

Now, vast amounts of information can be stored on tiny **computer chips**, as small as a grain of sand. These chips are easily hidden, but also easily stolen. People are tending more and more to store secret information in codes which are made up by a computer. They can only be unscrambled by the same computer.

This minature lapel microphone is just one of the ways spying has been made easier in the 1990s.

In 1900 most people conducted business by letter, or face to face. This was true of companies and ordinary people.

Business meetings

People did do business by letter. But it was very unusual for people to do business with people they had never met, or with a company they had never met a person from. People placed a lot of faith in face-to-face meetings and built up trust. When the leaders of various countries wanted to try to work out problems between their countries, they did not write. They sent representatives to meetings. They even arranged to meet personally in very serious situations.

Other business

If a person wanted money from a bank, they had to go there. They could write a cheque but the person who wanted to cash the cheque would have to go to the bank. Shopping had to be done in person. Workers had to go to work, unless they did work from home, but this work tended to be the worst paid kind of manual work, such as making matches or brushes by hand.

New Orleans businessmen bought and sold cotton. Many business people still wanted to see the quality of the goods before they bought them. They went down to the docks to look at the cotton and do business face to face.

Virtually face to face

People still like to meet face to face. Political leaders still meet in person to discuss important issues. But today people can meet face to face without travelling anywhere by using modern technology. Machines can send **digital** images of people around the world. They turn the pictures into a series of numbers, send them to another computer, which turns the numbers into the image again. A person can sit in an office in London and talk to people in Hong Kong, Melbourne and Chicago, face to face in a video conference. They can watch screens that show clear images of the speaker, so it is possible to watch their reactions, as well as hear them talk.

Computerized business

Now you can bank, shop, get insured, book a holiday and even consult the doctor by computer. As long as you have the technology, you need never leave home to do business again! A combination of **e-mail**, telephones, **faxes**, **ISDNs** and the Internet will let you do it all from home.

Working from home

Nowadays working from home is becoming more and more popular, especially with people who work mostly on computers. This has many advantages for the worker and the employer. The worker does not have to travel to work, so they avoid the problems of traffic and rush hour congestion. They can organize their working hours to suit themselves. Part-time home-workers may even be able to work without having to find childcare for their children. The employers do not have to provide office space, equipment or facilities such as canteens, for home-workers.

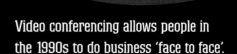

Video conferencing allows people in the 1990s to do business 'face to face'.

THE FUTURE?

With all the ways of sending images around the world, how will people keep in touch in the next century? Will they ever meet? How will they do business?

Remote trade

In 1998 the World Trade Organization (WTO) predicted a huge growth in the amount of trade done over the Internet, which would reduce the need to transport goods anywhere. Books, music, X-rays, pictures and films can all be sent over the Internet. In 1991 there were 4.5 million Internet users. The WTO predicts there will be over 300 million users by the year 2000, and billions by the year 2050.

News on the Net

The US journalist Charles Krauthemmer, who has made a study of communication technologies, predicted in *Scientific American* that newspapers as a way of communicating will not survive into the 21st century: '*The future of news is with the Net.*'

Personal news

Michio Kaku, author of *Visions*, suggested in 1998 that: '*by 2020 people will receive personal newspapers, selected from the Internet and tailored to their interests. They will supply the specific kinds of information that person needs from trusted sources.*'

This person is examining a brain scan which was sent to her computer screen by phone. This method means a doctor can give a diagnosis on a patient who lives thousands of miles away.

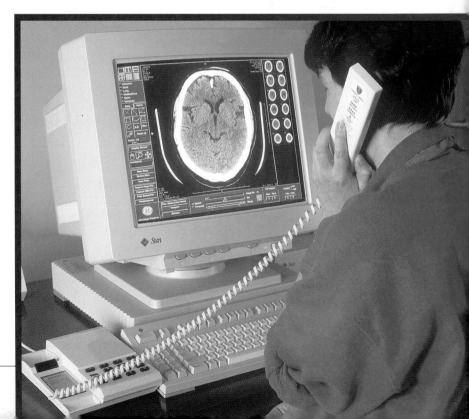

Space communications

Joseph N Pelton, Professor of Telecommunications at the University of Colorado, wrote in *Scientific American* that: '*Space-based telecommunications systems will provide rapid access to all types of information, from hand-held or briefcase-sized terminals anywhere on the planet. Mass **virtual reality** entertainment, videos on demand and expanding tele-health and tele-education systems are just some of the services that we can expect.*'

Communication **satellites,** like this, are released into space from space shuttles. The satellites are designed for voice, video and data communications.

People as machines?

Machines will not only run communications systems, they will, many people predict, become more and more involved in everyday activities. Perhaps machines will be implanted in people themselves. They will not only be the channel for communication, they will take part in the communicating process.

In 1997 a French futurology group, led by M Thierry Gaudin, predicted in *2100, recit du prochaine siecle*, that : '*Personal electronic payment cards will become so important that they may be implanted in the human body. So will a telecommunication chip, which will allow people to stay in touch all the time.*'

GLOSSARY

automatic/automated worked by machine, following a set pattern, not worked by people

code giving words and numbers different meanings to keep them secret

computer chips small pieces of silicon, part of a computer, that store and process electric signals

developed/developing countries developed countries (such as the USA) are rich, industrial countries. Developing countries began industrialization later, have less industry, and are not as rich.

digital a system of 1s and 0s, used to send and store information

e-mail electronic mail, sent from computer to computer by connectiong the computer to a telephone line using a tool called a modem

electromagnetic using electrical and magnetic fields

engravings pictures made by making lines on metal plates and using acid to eat away uncovered parts of the metal

exchange a place where various telephone lines meet and connections can be made between these lines

fax short for 'facsimilie transmission'. Faxes send messages over phone lines to produce an image of the information sent, just as it is, like a photo. You can fax handwriting, pictures and typed documents.

fibre optics thin, flexible, glass fibres that reflect light

frequency the level at which a sound is pitched, or how often it repeats in a second

hack to enter into a computer system illegally

impression a mark or shape made by pressing

ISDN the first letters of the words: International Standard Digital Network. ISDN uses telephone lines to send digital messages from one computer to another.

Morse Code   a code invented by Samuel Morse, in which each letter is represented by a combination of long and short signals – the signals or either sounds of flashes of light

operator   a person who works a piece of equipment

receiver   a piece of equipment that picks up signals

satellites   automatic machines that follow a fixed path in space, around the Earth

set   put into place

sorting office   a place where letters arrive from many postboxes and are sorted out according to the various place they are going to

steamships   ships powered by steam power, produced by burning coal or wood to make steam to drive the engine

switchboard   a place where telephone calls are picked up and moved on

telegraph   a way of sending messages by sending electric signals along wires over the ground or under the sea

terrestrial   working on Earth only

transmitter   a piece of equipment that sends up signals

type   a piece of wood or metal with a single letter carved into the surface

virtual reality   a system, usually using goggles and some form of headset, that tricks the brain into thinking that the images it shows are three-dimensional

wireless equipment   the parts that are needed to make a radio which sends electronic signals without wires

INDEX